D1074575

THE

Little Book

OF

HINDU
WISDOM

THE
Little Book
OF
HINDU
WISDOM

STEPHEN CROSS

ELEMENT

Shaftesbury, Dorset ✦ Rockport, Massachusetts
Melbourne, Victoria

Compiled by Stephen Cross

© ELEMENT BOOKS LIMITED 1997

Published in Great Britain in 1997 by
ELEMENT BOOKS LIMITED
Shaftesbury, Dorset SP7 9BP

Published in the USA in 1997 by
ELEMENT BOOKS INC.
PO Box 830, Rockport, MA 01966

Published in Australia in 1997 by
ELEMENT BOOKS
and distributed by
PENGUIN AUSTRALIA LTD
487 Maroondah Highway, Ringwood, Victoria 3134

Cover illustration: from the Gita Govinda, Garhwal, late 18th century

Designed by
BRIDGEWATER BOOKS

Printed and bound in Singapore
British Library Cataloguing in Publication data available
Library of Congress Cataloging in Publication data available

ISBN 1 86204 109 1

The publishers would like to thank the following for the use of pictures:
Bridgeman Art Library, e.t. archive.

FOREWORD

The wisdom offered in this little book is not tied
to a particular set of dogmas and beliefs, but is of a
kind which can be approached by men and
women of all sorts: 'If I were asked to define the
Hindu creed,' Mahatma Gandhi once observed,
'I should simply say, search after Truth through
non-violent means.'

Yet within these pages the reader will find,
drawn together from authentic sources, many of
the core ideas of the Hindu tradition. Like Indian
civilisation itself, these passages range across a vast
period of time, from the *Rig Veda* (composed at
the latest around 1200 B.C.E., and probably much
earlier) and the Upanishads (about 700 to 300 B.C.E.),
to the words of saints and teachers of the
nineteenth and twentieth centuries. Throughout
the whole of this period the tradition remains
consistent and unbroken.

Sometimes the teachings may seem, at first,
paradoxical or strange. Certainly they differ in
important respects from some of the views we
have grown used to in the West. But careful
thought about them will reveal their depth, and
their relevance to our lives.

There was not non-existent nor existent;
  there was no realm of air, no sky beyond it.
What covered in, and where? and what gave shelter?
  Was water there, unfathomed depth of water?

Who verily knows and who can here declare it,
  whence it was born and whence comes this creation?
The Gods are later than this world's production.
  Who knows then whence it first came into being?

He, the first origin of this creation,
  whether He formed it all or did not form it,
Whose eye controls this world in highest heaven,
  He verily knows it, or perhaps He knows not.

Rig Veda, 10.129

From the Creation Hymn of the *Rig Veda*. Several verses
have been omitted.

Seek the company of the good, for it is there
He has His dwelling place.

KABIR *(1440–1518)*

The Self (Atman), which is free from evil, ageless, deathless, sorrowless, hungerless, thirstless, whose desire is the Real, whose conception is the Real – He should be searched out, Him one should desire to understand.

Chandogya Upanishad, 8.7.1

He is the unseen Seer, the unheard Hearer, the unthought Thinker, the ununderstood Understander. Other than He there is no seer. Other than He there is no hearer. Other than He there is no thinker. Other than He there is no understander. He is your Soul (Atman), the Inner Controller, the Immortal.

Brihadaranyaka Upanishad, 3.7.23

Some look upon the Self as marvellous. Others speak of It as wonderful. Others again hear of It as a wonder. And still others, though hearing, do not understand It at all.

Bhagavad Gita, 2.29

It moves. It moves not.
It is far, and It is near.
It is within all this,
And It is outside of all this.

Isha Upanishad, verse 5

To attempt to think of the Self which is beyond the range of thought is only to create a new thought.

Ashtavakra Gita, 12.7

The Self is never knowable and is not directly denoted by any word.

SHANKARA (c. 700 C.E.)

"Bring hither a fig from there."

"Here it is, sir."

"Divide it."

"It is divided, sir."

"What do you see there?"

"These rather fine seeds, sir."

"Of these, please, divide one."

"It is divided, sir."

"What do you see there?"

"Nothing at all, sir."

Then he said to him:

"Verily, my dear, that finest essence which you do not perceive – verily, my dear, from that finest essence this great sacred fig tree thus arises. Believe me, my dear," said he, "that which is the finest essence – this whole world has that as its soul. That is Reality. That is Atman. That art thou."

Chandogya Upanishad, 6.12.1–3

Consciousness is pure, eternal and infinite: it does not arise nor cease to be. It is ever there in the moving and unmoving creatures, in the sky, on the mountain and in fire and air. When life-breath (*prana*) ceases, the body is said to be "dead" or "inert". The life-breath returns to its source – air – and consciousness freed from memory and tendencies remains as the self.

Yoga Vasishtha, 3.55

There is no greater mystery than this,
that being the Reality ourselves,
we seek to gain Reality.

SHRI RAMANA MAHARSHI *(1879–1950)*

14

What *is*, is the sole reality – which is neither created nor destroyed. It is that infinite consciousness that is perceived by the ignorant as the universe.

Yoga Vasishtha, 3.52

The unreal never is. The Real never is not. Men possessed of the knowledge of the Truth fully know both these.

Bhagavad Gita, 2.16

This Soul of mine within the heart is smaller than a grain of rice, or a barley-corn, or a mustard-seed, or a grain of millet, or the kernel of a grain of millet; this Soul of mine within the heart is greater than the earth, greater than the atmosphere, greater than the sky, greater than these worlds. Containing all works, containing all desires, containing all odors, containing all tastes, encompassing this whole world, the unspeaking, the unconcerned – this is the Soul of mine within the heart, this is Brahman. *

Chandogya Upanishad, 3.14.3-4

---

*   The ultimate Reality, the ground of the universe.

Ganez

And as, indeed, from fire the sparks do issue,
And likewise, too, from out the sun its light-rays,
From It repeatedly all breathing creatures
Come forth into this world, each in its order.

Maitri Upanishad, 6.26

As the rays of the sun differ not from the
sun, so matter differs not from God.

Avadhut Gita, 2.7

You are Brahman, I am Brahman, the whole
universe is Brahman. Whatever you are doing,
realise this truth at all times. This Brahman or the
self alone is the reality in all beings, even as clay is
the real substance in thousands of pots.

Yoga Vasishtha, 6.1.49

He is here,
And all these forms are His.
He is also not of the here;
And so, all these forms
Are shadows of the Formless.
God is of the here and not of the here;
These are his twin attributes.
But He is, here and beyond, endless. He is.

NAMMALVAR *(between 7th and 9th century C.E.)*

You should contemplate this truth again and again, from beginning to end, reflect upon it and you should march along this path now, O noble one. Though engaged in diverse activities, you will not be bound if your intelligence is saturated with this truth; otherwise, you will fall, even as an elephant falls from the cliff. Again, if you conceptualize this teaching for your intellectual entertainment and do not let it act in your life, you will stumble and fall like a blind man.

Yoga Vasishtha, 6.1.1

Creation is the rise of a false view of the real. World-manifestation is the persistence of that view, and world-dissolution is its removal.

SHRI SWAMI MANGALNATH *(d. 1930)*

Thou art woman. Thou art man.
Thou art the youth and the maiden too.
Thou as an old man totterest with a staff.
Being born, thou becomest facing in every
   direction.

Thou art the dark-blue bird and the green [parrot]
   with red eyes.
Thou hast the lightning as thy child. Thou art
   the seasons and the seas.
Having no beginning, thou dost abide with
   immanence,
Wherefrom all beings are born.

Shvetashvatara Upanishad, 4.3–4

Two birds, fast bound companions,
Clasp close the self-same tree.
Of these two, the one eats sweet fruit;
The other, looks on without eating. ★

Mundaka Upanishad, 3.1.1

★ The two birds are the real and the illusory self, Atman
and jiva. The tree is the body. The sweet fruit is worldly
experience.

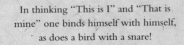

In thinking "This is I" and "That is
mine" one binds himself with himself,
as does a bird with a snare!

Maitri Upanishad, 6.30

I visited the garden, and was myself
The color and scent of every flower.
"My" and "Thy" have gone,
And hope and longing with them.
I alone remain.

SWAMI RAMA TIRTHA *(1873–1906)*

Seeing the gardener approaching, the buds cried out:
"Today the blossoms have been picked,
Tomorrow will be our turn."
As the woodcutter advanced, the trees sighed and said:
"It matters nothing to us that we are to be cut down,
But, alas, the birds will lose their homes."
As the potter was kneading the wet clay, it said:
"Today, O friend, thou art kneading me,
But tomorrow thou wilt have to make a bed in my lap."
Kabir saw a mill grinding the wheat and cried:
"Alas! No grain remains between the grinding stones,
Yet those that cling to the pivot are not destroyed."

KABIR *(1440–1518)*

As a goldsmith, taking a piece of gold, reduces it to
another newer and more beautiful form, just so this
soul, striking down this body and dispelling its
ignorance, makes for itself another newer and more
beautiful form.

Brihadaranyaka Upanishad, 4.4.4

Grace is within you. If it were
external, it would be useless.

SHRI RAMANA MAHARSHI
(1879–1950)

In a way, everyone is qualified. He who suffers is
qualified to be happy. He who knows that the
worldly objects, visible and invisible, have nothing
but sufferings to give, is qualified. He is not qualified
who still thinks that any worldly means whatsoever
can bring lasting happiness. Let him make vain
experiments until he is tired.

SHRI DADA OF ALIGARH *(1854–1910)*

Being ever-available, liberation has no birth and no origin; being ever-fixed, there is no action in it; being ever-pure, it admits of no process of purification; and as it is Self, how can it be the object of achievement?

SHRI SWAMI MANGALNATH (d. 1930)

Even as a man casts off worn-out clothes, and puts on others which are new, so the embodied casts off worn-out bodies, and enters into others which are new.

Bhagavad Gita, 2.22

What is the use of merely listening to lectures? The real thing is practice.

SHRI RAMAKRISHNA (1836–1886)

To the Brahmin who has known the Self, all the
Vedas are of so much use as a reservoir is when there
is a flood everywhere.

Bhagavad Gita, 2.46

There is no spiritual peace for the ignorant, because
they desire and seek it in the external world.

Ashtavakra Gita, 18.39

The forest of ignorance has numerous ant-hills
inhabited by deadly snakes in the form of
sense-cravings, many blind-holes known as death
and many forest-fires of sorrow; in it roam the
thieves of violence and greed, as also the most
deadly enemy of ego-sense.

Yoga Vasishtha, 5.35

गारगिगुजी श्रेष्ठः स्वच्छविविधबुधर्षीगुत्रा परमसुखरचतुजरा अंगे
रेद्वेनसुनावे श्रमराया थी हेनवजावे सुमनुनहि श्रीप्रकुलरष्ये जवरठेनवधी
नहरष्ये विरष्ये कृतिहाप्रकृतिसिगाति सेहा प्रतिवसनतनपद्विके नेसिसाम
रे वितनीमोचितवोरिके रिनिमेधमनारा ॥१३६॥

Thinking of objects, attachment to them is formed in a man. From attachment longing, and from longing anger grows. From anger comes delusion, and from delusion loss of memory. From loss of memory comes the ruin of discrimination, and from the ruin of discrimination he perishes.

Bhagavad Gita, 2.62–63

> *All action in its entirety…*
> *attains its consummation in knowledge.*
>
> *Bhagavad Gita, 4.33*

The spiritual path is for the liberal-minded and the miserly ones remain only on the fringe of it.

SHRI DADA OF ALIGARH *(1854–1910)*

One who has fallen into the stream of
births and deaths cannot save himself
by anything else except Knowledge.

SHANKARA *(c. 700 C.E.)*

> *Where there is "I" there is bondage,*
> *where there is no "I" there is release.*
>
> *Ashtavakra Gita, 8.4*

I bow to the bliss-giving feet of Shri Hari, *
By whose grace the cripple scales the highest mountains,
The blind can see, the deaf hear,
And the dumb discourse eloquently.
Surdas says: I take refuge in the grace of the Lord Hari,
Again and again I run for refuge to Him.

SURDAS *(16th century)*

---

* Hari is a name of Vishnu, and of his incarnation as Krishna.

A woman secretly carries on an intrigue with her lover. Live in the world like that woman, doing your many duties, with your soul secretly yearning for the Lord. She thinks of her lover all the time that she does her household duties.

SHRI RAMAKRISHNA *(1836–1886)*

Knowledge is like the bricks of which a house is built, and devotion is like the cement. You cannot build a house only with bricks, the building will collapse. The devotional aspect is the cement in between.

SHRI SWAMI SATHYANANDA OF VRINDAVAN
(contemporary)

Do you seek God? Well, seek Him in man!
His divinity is manifest more in man than in
any other object. Look around you for a man
with a love of God that overflows,
a man who yearns for God, a man
intoxicated with His love. In such a man
God has incarnated Himself.

SHRI RAMAKRISHNA *(1836–1886)*

Man must dwell in the world
untainted,
As the lotus dwells in the pond.

SWAMI RAMA TIRTHA *(1873–1906)*

May the world be peaceful. May the wicked become gentle. May all creatures think of mutual welfare. May their minds be occupied with what is auspicious. And may our hearts be immersed in selfless love for the Lord.

Bhagavata Purana 5.18.9

Attach yourself to the feet
Of Him who is void of all attachment.
That is the way to shed yours.

TIRUVALLUVAR *(between 7th and 9th century C.E.)*

When a devotee reaches a certain stage and
becomes fit for enlightenment, the same God who
he was worshipping comes as Guru and leads him
on. The Guru comes only to tell him, "God is
within yourself. Dive within and realize". God,
Guru and the Self (Atman) are the same.

SHRI RAMANA MAHARSHI *(1879–1950)*

If the splendor of a thousand suns were
to rise up simultaneously in the sky,
that would be like the splendour of
that Mighty Being.

Bhagavad Gita, 11.12

This seemingly endless stream of ignorance can be crossed over only by the constant company of the holy ones. From such company there arises wisdom concerning what is worth seeking and what is to be avoided. Then there arises the pure wish to attain liberation. This leads to serious enquiry. Then the mind becomes subtle because the enquiry thins out the mental conditioning.

Yoga Vasishtha, 3.122

Some people say the mind is an enemy within us. The mind is a friend also. Both are there. That is why they say, "Mind is the cause of bondage and also of liberation". If you put it in contact with the sense objects it will make for bondage. If you put it in contact with realized souls it will make for liberation.

SHRI SWAMI SATHYANANDA OF VRINDAVAN
(contemporary)

41

How the screen of Maya *
Is spread out in brilliant colours!
How it vibrates with energy
In swirling waters and solid stone!
Lakes, islands, bays and seas,
Mountains and deserts, states and cities,
The young and the old,
The land and its inhabitants,
Prophets and holy books,
The whole earth and sky,
Horses, elephants, slaves,
Kings and overlords of empires,
All are depicted on the canvas of Maya.
How this cobweb gleams and sparkles,
Though its threads are only our dreams!

SWAMI RAMA TIRTHA *(1873–1906)*

---

* The illusory world-appearance existing in the mind.

> *When you are climbing the ladder,*
> *don't forget the rungs.*
>
> SHRI SWAMI SATHYANANDA OF VRINDAVAN
> *(contemporary)*

The wise ones declare that the mind is caused by
the movement of prana;* and hence by the restraint
of prana, the mind becomes quiescent. When the
mind abandons the movement of thought, the
appearance of the world-illusion ceases. The movement of prana is arrested at the moment when all
hopes and desires come to an end in one's heart.

Yoga Vasishtha, 5.78

---

* Breath understood as the animating principle.

Consider the matter sincerely
And you will see that it is yourselves
Who have created Kali Yug.★
The notion "I am not God"
Is Kali Yug.
"I am the body" is Kali Yug.
"The body is the Self" is Kali Yug.
Materialism is Kali Yug.

SWAMI RAMA TIRTHA *(1873–1906)*

★   The last and worst age of a cycle of creation, said to be the
    present period.

*The wise know that all that is not the Self is
merely a movement of the mind.*

Ashtavakra Gita 18.7

SOURCES

The text is drawn from the following sources. While every effort has been made to secure permissions, if there should be any errors or oversights regarding copyright material, we apologize and will make suitable acknowledgment in any future edition.

The following translations of Hindu texts have been used:

Rig Veda – R.T.H. Griffith, *The Hymns of the Rig Veda* (1889). Reprint: Motilal Banarsidass, Delhi, 1986.

Upanishads – R.E. Hume, *The Thirteen Principal Upanishads*. Oxford University Press. Reprinted 1962.

Bhagavad Gita – Swami Swarupananda (1909). Reprint: Advaita Ashrama, Calcutta, 1989.

Yoga Vasishtha – Swami Venkatesananda, *Vasistha's Yoga*. State University of New York Press, 1993.

Ashtavakra Gita – Hari Prasad Shastri. Shanti Sadan, London 1949.

Avadhut Gita – Hari Prasad Shastri. Shanti Sadan, London 1968.

Bhagavata Purana – C. Goswami & M. Sastri, *Srimad, Bhagavata Mahapurana*. Gita Press, Gorakhpur, India, 1982.

Quotations from individual sources are from the following books:

Shankara – Swami Jagadananda (trans.), *Upadesa Sahasri*, Sri Ramakrishna Math, Mylapore, Madras, 1979.

Nammalvar, Tirumazhisai Alvar, and Tiruvalluvar – A. Srinivasa Raghavan (trans.), 'Alwars', in *Devotional Poets and Mystics*, Ministry of Information & Broadcasting, Delhi, 1983.

Kabir and Surdas – Hari Prasad Shastri (trans.), *Indian Mystic Verse*, Shanti Sadan, London, 1984.

Shri Dada of Aligarh – Hari Prasad Shastri, *The Heart of the Eastern Mystical Teaching*, Shanti Sadan, London.

Shri Ramakrishna – *Condensed Gospel of Sri Ramakrishna*, Sri Ramakrishna Math, Mylapore, Madras, 1986.

Shri Ramana Maharshi – *Erase the Ego*, Bharatiya Vidya Bhavan, Bombay, 1974.

Shri Swami Mangalnath – Hari Prasad Shastri (trans.), *Triumph of a Hero*, Shanti Sadan, London, 1961.

Shri Swami Sathyananda – 'Words of Shri Swami Sathyananda', *Self-Knowledge: a Yoga Quarterly*, vol. 40, nos. 3 & 4, Shanti Sadan, London, 1989.

Swami Rama Tirtha – A.J. Alston (trans.), *Yoga and the Supreme Bliss*. Privately published; available from Shanti Sadan, London.